MINDING MY OWN BUSINESS 2

SIMPLE STEPS TO START YOUR BUSINESS.

Introduction:

Many people today want to start a business for many different reasons. Whether their motivation is to make unlimited amounts of income, freedom of time, or to showcase their passions and gifts to the world. The entrepreneur journey can be what you make of it. It can provide many helpful resources for you and your family. Being an entrepreneur can also be stressful if you do not know where to start, but the rewards are very unlimited. Being able to monetize on my gifts and talents while sharing them with the world has been one of my greatest accomplishments. I am sure you have heard Madam CJ Walker story. Walker was an African American entrepreneur, philanthropist, and political and social activist. Walker made her fortune thanks to her homemade line of hair care products for Black women. She is just one of the many examples of how you can succeed in entrepreneurship. Everything you need to be a successful and legal business will be discovered throughout this book. You might be someone that doesn't really have a clue as to what you would like to do as far as business. Or you may be someone that has talent and just does not know how to showcase it to the world to make a profit. Whatever your drive was for choosing to read this book I am hopeful that this book will help you discover your hidden gifts and talents so that you can start a successful business.

As you read and learn about how to start and legalize your business, you will also learn:

Table of Contents

- The benefits of having a business (page 4)
- What is needed to be considered a legal business? (page 31)
- How to register your business (page 39)
- How to get your EIN (page 41)
- How to get a professional website with little or no money (page 43)
- Business Card (page 46)
- Discover Business bank accounts. (page 49)
- Develop business credit. (page 51)
- Getting trade lines for your business (page 54)
- Marketing your business (page 57)
- All about loans, grants, and contracts (page 70)
- Why are taxes made for businesses. (page 82)
- Beneficial Ownership Report (page 83)
- Government Contracting (page 85)

Source 1: The benefits of having a business:

      There are many benefits of having your own business. Although there are pros and cons, just like with anything else, we will talk about the good, and not so good parts of having your own business. I believe the good parts of owning a business trumps the bad. Some of the great benefits of owning your own business includes, choosing your customers, having more time for things you want to do, creating a product or a service that you are knowledgeable of, hiring people that you would love to work with, and most importantly creating the income that you would like to have with no cap.

(Choose your own customers)

 I know you are probably thinking, how do I choose my own customers within my business? I am glad you asked. Choosing your customers could be beneficial for you whether you are providing a product or a service. Your services could include some type of class, a mentorship program or showing someone how to do something, like, how to build credit, doing make-up, selling homes, etc. With certain types of services, you can interview your clients and size them up to determine if your services are right for them. This also has a lot to do with how and where you are marketing your services or products. You must ask yourself when you are looking to work with a client, what type of customers do I want to attract?

There are different types of customers, but I am going to tell you about the 4 types of customers.

First on the list is **Price buyers**. These customers want to buy products and services only at the lowest possible price. They are less concerned about value, differentiation, or relationships. A price buyer customer will look for discounts before they do a dealing with you. For example, if you sell candy bars for $2 and they found someone else that sales an off brand for $1.95, they will be more willing to go with the $1.95 candy bar, even if the service is not as great as yours. These are not bad customers; you just need to make sure that you are beating your competitors in pricing.

The next customer is **Relationship buyers.** These customers want to trust and have dependable relationships with their suppliers, and they expect suppliers to take good care of them. Relationship buyers is some of my best customers in my personal businesses. They will continue to support you because you have developed a relationship with them. You should always give these types of customers discounts because they will always buy more, and in most cases bring you more business. To develop a relationship with this type of customer you need to be available whenever they have a question or concern. I know that we are moving into a technology era and most of your customer service duties may be computer generated, the relationship buyers want to feel like they are connected to you personally. With these customers, I may call and check on them personally just to say hi. Not trying to sell or push a sell on them. Doing this builds a relationship which allows me to make more money and provide outstanding services to the customers.

The third type of customer is a **Value buyer.** These customers understand value and want suppliers to be able to provide the most value in their relations. If you have a product or service, make sure that it is quality. This customer will pay top dollar if the value is there and reflect the service or products they are buying. With this customer you want to be careful and be on your game. If you are not providing value, this customer will tell others and ruin your business. My practices are to always provide value and good customer service. Also, with this customer be sure that your product or service is not overpriced. They will also look around and measure the value of other sellers before buying.

Poker player buyers. These are relationship or value buyers who have learned that if they act like a price buyer, they can get high value for low prices. They come for relationship and value. At times they may wait for your price to drop, but they will always be loyal customers. Remember that the secret to choosing your client is in your pricing and marketing.

As you develop your prices, keep in mind that your marketing determines which type of customers you would like to service.

Time Freedom)

Another benefit of having your own business is the flexibility of having control of your own time. Time is something that you cannot get back. So, try not to waste it. Having control of your own time could mean spending more time with family and friends, vacationing and so much more. When you have time freedom, no one is going to tell you to get back to work or force you to do things you do not want to do on their time. You are in control of your time when you start your business. Managing your own time can have an upside and a downside. The upside as mentioned before is not having to work when you do not want to. But the downside is, taking too much time off. There is a good reason for stating this. If you own your own business and do not set time management, you can easily lose focus. Losing focus leads to losing customers, then business, which leads to not making money. You see it will be a ripple effect. It is very imperative that you manage your time and stay focused. I would like to say, although we work for ourselves, we still work for our customers. Without them you will not be in business. If you are reading this book, I assume that you have a business, or you are looking to start one. Please note that when you start a new business, you will not be on your own time yet. Having time to yourself comes later. Right now, it is all about the hustle of getting everything started correctly. Keep in mind, although you will be hustling day to day, it is important to also take certain days off. Taking days off will allow you to reset and not get burned out.

Below, I will list how to manage your time according to, Beeketing a Blog by Michelle.

1 – Schedule, if possible, everything! You can't trust your memory. Even if we believe we are keeping in mind all the things that we need to do accurately, most often than not, we might have forgotten something or misremembered an important detail. For busy entrepreneurs, you can't diminish the value of writing down, if possible, every task at hand. Find what works for you. You can either be more traditional by keeping a pocket notebook that you can always carry around or keep an online calendar. There are plenty of time management and scheduling calendar services online, like, Google Calendar. But there are more cool hacks and under-the-radar features that you can use to make your life in Google Calendar much easier to organize.

2 – The 2-Minute Rule Procrastination is a very common time wastage. For some entrepreneurs, delaying or postponing a task is sometimes because of the lack of focus or thinking that they still have plenty of time. Remember, time is not your friend. Most of the time it's just that you don't want to start. The 2-Minute Rule can help overcome your procrastination and laziness. Here's how: for any of your task that you're delaying, start just devoting two minutes of your time. If you need to craft a letter, just write two or three sentences in two minutes, and you'll find yourself finishing the entire letter. Want to finish your budget and expense report? Try logging your records, and you'll end up completing it in no time. The 2-Minute Rule doesn't always have to be finishing the task entirely, it's more on the process of starting the work. Don't waste your time figuring out when to start, but rather use this time in **taking action.**

3 – Attention Management We said earlier that in time management, the key is not about getting more and more time. It's mostly regarding how you change your attitude to manage your time. In managing your time, attention and focus are very crucial. Be alert. Why? This is because even if you allocate a portion of your time for a specific task but spend it switching from one task or another, it will be more likely that you will end up with a mediocre result. The way you control your focus and attention impacts directly your productivity. If you are too distracted by different internal and external affairs, your productivity will deplete, and the quality of your work will suffer. This creates more error and eats up more time fixing them. Thus, you'll already be wasting more time than usual.

4 – Prioritization and Delegation. I'm sure you know how distractions can negatively impact your quality and productivity. Distractions can be anything from small to big things or from within or outside your control. Anything that disrupts your work schedule is a distraction. This is when prioritization and delegation come in. Prioritization is learning when to say "no" to the things that don't really need your attention. While delegation is transferring those non-priority things to the more appropriate individuals. If you can, getting a personal assistant is the best way to delegate your scheduling and other administrative tasks and routines that eat up most of your time, which prevent you from focusing on the most important aspects of your business. The Prioritization & Delegation Matrix above will help you sort your tasks according to the following: Must Do: tasks that require your full attention and have serious repercussions when not completed immediately. Should Do: tasks that only require your monitoring so you can delegate. These tasks have serious repercussions when not completed immediately. Would Do – tasks that require your full attention and have moderate to no repercussions when not completed immediately. Usually, they can be done later. Could Do – tasks that you don't have to do so you can delegate. These tasks have moderate to no repercussions when not completed immediately.

5 – Allocate Unstructured Time. Unstructured time is exactly what it looks like, it is a time allocated for nothing. By "nothing", it's anything aside from a work agenda or a personal meeting. Unstructured time is your "me time". But you'll probably be thinking: "I'm already busy, why do I have to allocate time for nothing"? However, your unstructured or "slack" time is an important aspect of effective time management. Why? The more time you put into your schedule, the busier you get. And the busier you get, the more you push yourself into physical and mental exhaustion, and ultimately, burnout or even sickness. As an entrepreneur, your health is your wealth. Your unstructured time can be used for a one to two hours nap time. It can be weekly or every other day. The point is it's the time when your brain is free to wander which allows you to be more imaginative, refreshed, and stressed-free. Thus, having more energy, attention, and focus on work.

6 – Conduct a Time Audit. Do you really know how much time you spend on a particular task? Do you follow your schedule, or do you always find yourself extending a meeting, so the rest of your schedule is messed up? Time audit enables you to pinpoint which task eats up more time than allocated. You can conduct a time audit using this form below to identify potential drains on your time. Answer as honest as possible and put all your tasks and actions that you're normally doing daily. Include anything from work schedule to personal actions like social media or phone usage. Then, categorize them according to the Prioritization & Delegation Matrix. The 'Saved Time' portion allows a glimpse of how much time you are saving or wasting. A negative number means the task has been performed longer than allotted. You can also sum up the 'Time Spent' column and do a pivot of the category to identify which category you're spending most of your time with. For instance, the chart above shows that 'Should Do' tasks and activities topped the most time spent in a day. This means that you're not really managing your time accordingly because these activities can be delegated.

7. Find Ways to Automate. Working hard doesn't equate to the number of hours spent. Instead, working hard means working effectively and smarter. Smart entrepreneurs don't have to spend manual laborious hours to get things ended. They use technology to their advantage. Gone are the days when you must manually input or extract your data before you can try and analyze your store's performance. There are already readily available platforms that can automate your store's analysis using various types of analytics. What you need to do is find what processes or activities you can invest in automation to help you save time. Moreover, your head may be filled with hundreds of tasks, plans, and business concerns being an entrepreneur. When it comes to clearing your mind of too many tasks, you can take help from some of the amazing time management apps. These apps help you streamline your work and be more productive. In addition, when it comes to handling things like contracts, invoices, and proposals, you may need to find yourself an automation app, like Hello Bonsai, to save you a ton of time and effort. Hello Bonsai, a freelancing management app, offers freelance proposals and contracts. It handles your freelance invoices and payments; helps you track your expenses and manage your clients & leads.

8. Spend your time wisely. No matter how trivial or important a task or activity is, they all affect your overall time management. What's more crucial in effective time management is not about how much time you have, but how you make use of that time. That's why we've shown you different tips to spend your time wisely. Your head may be filled with hundreds of tasks, plans, and business concerns being an entrepreneur. When it comes to clearing your mind of too many tasks, you can take help from some of the amazing time management apps. These apps help you streamline your work and be more productive. They not only save a lot of time but also help you collaborate better with your team, be it in-office or remote. *(Source: beeketing.com/blog/time-management-tips-entrepreneurs/ © Beeketing Blog)*

Again, time freedom is the number one reason why people start their own businesses. Time is the only thing we cannot get back as people. Time never stops. You ever hear someone say, "time is not your friend?" This statement is somewhat true. Time is not your friend. But it could be if you use it before it uses you. Learn to manage your time here on earth and help others. This will help you achieve financial freedom.

(Offer the right product or service that comes naturally to you.)

Offering a product that comes naturally to you can be very beneficial to you in your process. You want to offer something that you are skilled in or have a plethora of knowledge in. For example, if you are good at saving money and budgeting, you may want to offer a service that helps other people with financial budgeting. If you are good at handling money, create a course for your customers to follow from beginning to end. You can help them decide what they need to do to get to their 5–10-year goals. Another example could be, if you are good with doing make-up and you have the knowledge, you can offer classes that shows others how to achieve the look they want. Or maybe you are skilled in coming up with business plans. If so, you can learn to be a business planner. The point is, do something that comes natural to you. Customers are more likely to trust you when you show confidence in what you are selling. You can build this confidence by increasing your knowledge of your products or services. Do your research. I believe even if you feel like you are a pro at your products or services, you should still increase your knowledge. I attend a workshop every 6 months just to sharpen my skills. It is important to know that you will never stop learning as a business owner.

Hire the people you want to work with:

Another reason why you may want to start your own business is the ability to employ people that you want. Yes, you can absolutely hire the people that you like, only if you think they are right for your business. You are the boss. Starting out you may not need employees, but as you grow your business you will need to start delegating some responsibility to others. Doing so will allow you to scale your business and grow your business. When you are hiring people to work in your company you want to be sure that they will be an asset and not a liability. This means, you want someone that can handle the responsibility without you looking over their shoulder. Sometimes, this may be someone you know and trust. In most cases, it may be one of your family members.

I know that it is a myth that hiring family members or friends in your business is not a good idea, but the choice is yours. If your family or friend understands the direction that your business is going in and they learn that customer service is the number one thing that will keep your business going, then they may be good employees. On the other hand, if they have toxic traits, such as showing up late, bad attitudes, and not caring about the services your business provides, you will end up losing customers, money, and maybe even worse. This is never a good thing.

Assets are the items your company owns that can provide future economic benefit. Liabilities are what you owe other parties. In short, assets put money in your pocket, and liabilities take money out! Your employees can be considered assets or liabilities depending on what and if they solve a problem for you and your business. The way you know if you have hired an asset, or a liability is if an employee makes you money or takes money out of your pocket. I like to say, if an employee saves or makes me money and save me time, they are considered an asset. But if they cost me money by making too many mistakes, not being on time with deadlines, or I always need to go back to their work, then they are a liability. I do not know about you, but I would rather have assets any day. Furthermore, it is said that an employee who is related to you might assume they have special privileges. This could be a problem. They might try to abuse you and your business. This could mean, if you sell products, they might feel entitled to get products for free all the time. But at the same time, it's easy for you to take advantage of your relatives and set higher expectations for them. You might exploit them into working more or taking less pay. Every startup business has different levels. You probably thought of hiring a family because you do not really have enough funds to hire outside help just yet. If this is the case, make sure that they know that this will be short term just to help you get off the ground. I would suggest that you only work with family if you have decided to start a family-owned business, and everyone involved is equal partners in the business. Always remember when it's time to grow your business, hiring someone that can save you money and make you money in your business is the goal.

Create your own income:

The last and the most important reason why many people start their own business is the freedom to make their own paychecks. I know this sounds crazy and impossible, but it is not. Whenever you get hired for a job your wage is determined for you whether you know it or not. Your job sets how much they think you are worth depending on the job you apply for. This is because every organization has budgets. No matter how long you work for a particular job, there is a glass ceiling which determines how far in the company you can go and how much money you can make. I am not against having a job, but you should be working to plan your exit someday.

What is a glass ceiling? The term glass ceiling refers to a metaphorical invisible barrier that prevents certain individuals from being promoted to managerial- and executive-level positions within an organization or industry. In short, the glass ceiling keeps you from achieving to much success in the workplace. My mentor would always tell me, "You will never get rich working for someone else". He understood the glass ceiling.

Now that we have discovered the glass ceiling, let's continue with the subject of creating your own income. In your business you determine how much your products or services will cost to the public, which translates to writing your own paycheck. You can decide to charge hundreds for your products or thousands of dollars for your services. You decide this. There is no glass ceiling. If you do the work and get the customers, the sky is not the limit. You have the world at your disposal. Your prices will always change; therefore, no one is coming to tell you how much to charge. You are the Boss. Starting out, you should test different prices and determine what prices gets the most customers. Keep in mind, no matter what your price is someone will always buy. You can decide how much money you want to make each year, each month, each day, or each hour. For Example, if you provide a service and the service you provide is $200, you only need 20 customers a month to make $4000. You need to decide how much you want to make. The good news is that there are no glass ceilings. If you want to make $40,000 a month, it is possible.

What You Need to Have a Legal Business

Source 2: What Do I Need to Have Legal Business?

Legalizing your business is the most important task that many new creators don't do. This is the first step after you have come up with your business name. After this, be sure that the business name you have chosen is not taken. You do not want to be the person who falls in love with a certain name and find that you cannot use it. I suggest you do a google search to see if your business name pulls up. If your business name is pulled up, there is a good chance that name is already taken by someone else. You also may want to do a search on the IRS website at, **(irs.gov).**

Get a Business Address

After you have searched and verified that your business name is clear, there is one step you need to take before you pay to register your business name. You need to get a **business**

address and phone number. This is an important step before you form your entity. The reason you need to get a business address before you register your business is more than just getting in position to qualify for business funding, but to have the correct information on your certificate of formation or your (LLC). The biggest mistake I've made when forming my first business is not putting another address (business address) while submitting my paperwork. This is a mistake that most people make. The address that you use on your certificate of formation will be shown in public records. Meaning, if you put a home address on the certificate, you may have customers and strangers coming to your home. This could be dangerous. To avoid these problems, you want to use **a virtual address,** if you do not have a physical store front. I know you are probably wondering, what is a virtual address and how do I get one? A **virtual office** is part of the flexible workspace industry that provides businesses with any combination of services, space and/or technology, without those businesses bearing the capital expenses of owning or leasing a traditional office. There are many platforms where you can obtain a business virtual address. *Ipostal.com* is a great platform where you can get a virtual business address and a business phone number. Ipostal.com allows you to choose the city and state where you would like your business address to be located. A good rule is to verify the addresses before you select one. It is best to choose an address that is not a store front postal center. Try to get an address that is connected to an office building. I've found that these locations work best when banks are searching for your businesses to approve you for funding. **Never use a PO Box.** Using a PO Box will flag your business and make it hard to get business funding. Although your virtual business address is a PO Box, you need to present you and your business like you rent out the location. If you do not obtain a business address before you register your entity, there are fees you will pay to make corrections on your certificate of formation. I am telling you this from my experience, so you do not make this mistake, or need to backtrack, and pay additional fees.

Determine which business entity is best for you

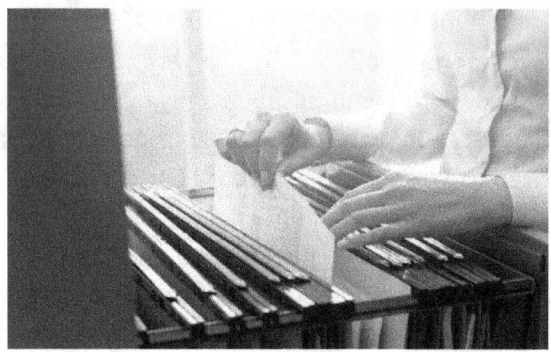

What are the different business entities?

You must decide which entity type would be the best formation for you and your business. There are different types of formations that you can use to legalize your business. I will discuss the main formations, which are: sole proprietorship, limited liability company (LLC), and corporation. Each has its own distinct advantages and disadvantages, depending on what you and your business need. For most of you reading this book an LLC may be the best for you as you start on your journey.

The first formation is sole proprietorship, also known as a sole tradership, individual entrepreneurship or proprietorship, is a type of enterprise owned and run by one person and in which there is no legal distinction between the owner and the business entity. This formation does not keep you from being separated from your "Business". For example, if someone gets sick from your baking business, they can sue you directly. This means you are fully liable. No separation from you or your business.

A limited liability company (LLC) is the US-specific form of a private limited company. It is a business structure that can combine the pass-through taxation of a partnership or sole proprietorship with the limited liability of a corporation. This formation separates you from your business. For example, if you have a baking business and someone gets food poising, they can only sue the business. They cannot sue you. This entity also allows you to get tax write-offs.

An S corporation (S Corp) for United States federal income tax, is a closely held corporation that makes a valid election to be taxed under Subchapter S of Chapter 1 of the Internal Revenue Code. In general, S corporations do not pay any income taxes. S corporations are corporations that elect to pass corporate income, losses, deductions, and credits through to their shareholders for federal tax purposes. To be an S-Corp you must be able to pay yourself a livable wage. I know you are probably thinking to yourself, I can do that. But be careful, there are many tax laws. I would suggest only creating a corporation if you are making enough money on paper to support all the tax rules, because if not you can end up paying fines from the IRS. If your business has income left over after you pay yourself a reasonable salary, then you should consider electing S-Corp tax status.

   A C corporation (C- Corp), under United States federal income tax law, is any corporation that is taxed separately from its owners. A C corporation is distinguished from an S corporation, which generally is not taxed separately. This entity is for big business with employees. When it comes to C Corps think of businesses like McDonalds, etc. You will pay double the taxes. C-corps are subject to double taxation while LLCs, S-corporations, and Partnerships are pass-through entities.

HOW TO REGISTER YOUR BUSINESS

Register your Business

After you have determined which business entity is best for you let's get it legalized. Meaning, you need to have your business registered with your secretary of state. Many businesses miss out on funding opportunities because they do not really have a legit business recognized by their state. If you are selling clothes as a side hustle, start a business and register your business with the Secretary of State so you can benefit from all the great things that business owners benefit from. Depending on the state that you live in, the cost to have your business legalized could range from $100 to $400. You can register your business on the secretary of state website at irs.gov, or you can use *legalzoom.com* and they will do everything for you. Legal Zoom will charge a filing fee for doing this for you, keep this in mind. Filing could take between 5-20 days depending on the service you select. You can also register a business in many states. If you decide to do this, be sure to do research on the state you are registering your business in. Taxes per state business license may differ. I suggest you start your first business in the state you live in. You will still be able to sell and offer services in other states.

HOW TO GET AN EIN

Get your EIN.

After you have determined the name of your business and you have registered your business with the secretary of state you should file for an E I N number, this is your business *Employee Identification Number.* I like to tell people this is like your business Social Security number. This number can be summoned from the Secretary of State website. I suggest that you wait 3 days before you apply for your EIN just to be sure everything is good with your entity registration. When you create an E IN you are telling the government that you have created another entity other than yourself. The great thing about this is that if you can't get certain things with your personal credit using your SSI, most creditors allow you to use an EIN number to help fund certain things for your business. In certain cases, some creditors will still use your personal Social Security number assigning you as a cosigner for your business. You will only be able to use one E IN number per business that is registered. Meaning, if you want to have more than one business, each registered business needs their own EIN number. Currently I have three LLCs with three different EIN numbers. This is a great benefit because the more entities I create the more funding I have access to.

CREATE YOUR WEBSITE AND BUSINESS EMAIL!

Business website and Business email

Having a business website is super important. Your business website shows that you are a legitimate business and gives you more credit in the eyes of customers and financial companies. There are many websites where you can build your own website for little to no money. **Wix.com, Godaddy.com, Bigcommerce.com, or shopify.com** are all good just to name a few. You can also hire an expert on these sites to create your business website for you. Having a website will give people all around the world access to you and your business. I was able to sell all over the USA and in two other countries because I have websites. Remember, you can be creative while building your site. This is all about what you like and how you want to represent your business. I recommend searching other companies' websites to get a clue as to how they are displaying their products or services. You will need to register your business domain name which should be www.(youbusinessname.com). One of mine for example is, www.noahsartamdp.com. This is how people will find you. You should also create a business email address. You can do this through some of these platforms or through google. A business email address will set you apart from other businesses that are using, (@gmail.com, @yahoo.com etc.) You want your email to be the same as your business. This shows your professionalism. So if you have a business that is called **Sherry Sweets, your website should be,** www.sherrysweets.com **and your email should be,** info@sherrysweets.com**, or** contact@sherrysweets.com. Everything needs to be uniform. This is the start to a successful business.

After this is done and you have a business address that is not a PO Box, you can then get a **google my business profile**. This will allow you to be found on google which ultimately increases your chances to find customers.

Next list your business in the 411 directories at *listyourself.net*. This will help your business to create a footprint.

Your business cards should outline your business

Business Cards:

     Business cards are a must. You want to be as professional as possible while you are building your business. There are many programs you can use to create your business cards. You want to have your business email, the name of your business, a little of what you sell or provide, social media sites, websites, and contact information on your business cards. You can make your business cards using sites such as canva.com or Vistaprint.com, just to name a few. Now you can also provide a QR code on your business card so potential customers can scan and go. This should be a simple process. Your business card is a preview of your website. I suggest you color coordinate your cards with your website. Also do research on certain colors. For example, if you want a more luxurious feel and look, you may decide to use black, gold, or purples. These colors show strength, sexiness, and boldness. This should be fun as you think of what you want to display to the world. I would suggest doing some research on certain colors which will attract customers. I've learned, most major companies use certain colors to attract customers. For Example: Fast food restaurants such as, McDonalds, Chick-Fila, Wendy's all use red and white as a base color. Rain is a warm color that makes food look more vibrant in Alberta and it can also increase appetite. White can be associated with cleanliness in simplicity. Now look at some of the banks like Chase Bank, PNC Bank, Bank of America, just to name a few. These companies use colors like red, white, and Blue. Blue signifies trust. Banks want their customers to trust them. So do your research and think of colors that go within the industry that you are entering.

Getting a Business Bank Account to Fit Your Needs.

Get a Business Bank Account

A business bank account is a must. Having one will allow you to get hundreds and thousands of dollars in business funding. If you have a personal credit score of 650 and above, most banks will offer you funding after you open a business account the same day. To open a business bank account, you will need the following: Your business certificate of filing, business address, website, EIN. Some banks may require less. The process usually takes 60 minutes to complete. Make sure you have all your documents before you go to the bank. If you have less than perfect credit, I suggest you open a bank account through the mid-size banks such as **PNC, BB&T, First Convenience Bank**. If you believe you are ready for the bigger banks like **Chase, Bank of America, or Wells Fargo,** you can open your accounts there. Whichever bank you decide to go with, they all have business funding options. After you have opened your business bank account you should start depositing money in it. If you are working a full-time job, you can start putting money from your job into your business bank account. This will allow the banks to see that you are using the account and have money coming through it. You can also start paying your expenses like car note, rent, and more out of this account. You are a business now so most of these expenses will be considered business write-offs. This is a whole different topic.

START BUILDING BUSINESS CREDIT.

Building Business Credit

      Most of us are in business to learn how to get business credit so we can grow, expand, and build wealth. In business you have 3 credit bureaus. There is Dun & Bradstreet, Experian Business, and Equifax Business. These bureaus score your business based on how your business pays back debt. I know you are probably wondering, why do I want to build business credit? Building business credit can open so many doors for you and your future. I know a lot of businesses that do not know about building business credit or how to use business credit. Business credit and personal credit are two different things. Let me explain. Bank will give more funding to a business than an individual. If you apply for a credit card on your personal credit and the banks give you a $500 limit and you use $450 of that card, your personal credit score will drop tremendously. Due to the utilization being high. But in business, if the banks give you $5000 for example and you use the whole $5000, your personal score is not affected and your business score is not affected. Banks know that business may use the max of the credit to keep the business running, so there are no penalties. In most cases you can pay back the business debt in 30 days, 60 days, or 90 days, depending on the type of loan or credit it is. Some of the best loans to get are business term loans. With some of these loans can be anywhere from $1000- $1,000,000. Some of these loans you may not need to start making payments on them for years. Remember, when it is time to pay back the loan, you can always pay the minimum balance to keep your business in good standing with the bureaus.

What is a Duns Number? The Data Universal Numbering System, abbreviated as DUNS or D-U-N-S, is a proprietary system developed and managed by Dun & Bradstreet that assigns a unique numeric identifier, referred to as a "DUNS number" to a single business entity. It was introduced in 1963 to support D&B's credit reporting practice. You can get the dun's number for *free at dnb.com.*

After you get your free DUNS number you can wait a few days and look for net accounts so you can start building business credit. You have different tiers with building business credit. You want to have at least 3 - 5 net 30 accounts to generate a paydex score. A **Paydex score** is your business credit score. You will get a paydex score by buying something from companies who have net programs and paying your bills back within the time allowed.

NET ACCOUNTS

What is a Net Account and how do I Get them?

A net 30 account is 30-day trade credit on invoices for business purchases, also known as a net30 tradeline or vendor tradeline. Net30 accounts offered by vendors extend credit to customers with net 30 terms. Business customers timely pay for purchases without interest charges. In short, net accounts can come in 30-, 60-, or 90-day accounts. Furthermore, if you buy something you can be granted a net 30 account, meaning you need to be able to pay it back within 30 days. Same with 60 and 90 paybacks at that time. You can get the net 30 accounts *from Grainger.com, Quill.com, Crownofficesupplies.com, uline.com.* Each of these vendors have different standards to getting net 30 accounts. After you have paid your net 30 accounts consistently for a few months, you can then go to tier 2 accounts which are business Gas cards, Home Depot Cards, and so many others.

Lastly, Tier 3 accounts are the business credit cards and higher business loans. Also tier 3 accounts can be car loans purchased through your business or real estate.

After all these steps, you should create a **Nav.com** account. Nav is an online company that provides business and personal credit reporting accounts. Its basic plan offers free access to a multitude of tools, including credit reports. The company also offers paid services, like identity theft protection and more detailed reporting. You will use this account to view your business scores.

MARKETING FOR MY BUSINESS

How to Market my business and increase sales

Marketing your business is one of the important things to do. There are many free resources you can research to help you with marketing. Website Search engine optimization is the process of improving the quality and quantity of website traffic to a website or a web page from search engines. SEO targets unpaid traffic rather than direct traffic or paid traffic. This is something that you can set up through your website. There are also ads you can run on social media or paid advertising. In my business I use paid advertising through google. This can be very expensive depending on your budget. If you decide to use google to advertise your business, I suggest that you hire a google expert to help you get your products or services on to the google platform. I prefer to google over any other platform because google is the number one search engine that allows customers to find you without you doing a lot of work. You must get your business out to the world so you can reach and help as many people as possible that you can.

8 steps to marketing your business according to Small Business Development Corporation:
www.smallbusiness.wa.gov.au/marketing/8-steps-to-marketing

Step 1

Conduct market research.

Market research is a key part of developing your marketing strategy. It is about collecting information that provides an insight into your customers' thinking, buying patterns, and location. In addition, market research can also assist you to undertake an initial sales forecast, monitor market trends and keep an eye on what your competition is doing.

Step 2

Profile your target markets!

Trying to promote your product or service to everyone can be costly and ineffective. Grouping or segmenting your potential customers based on certain characteristics will help to focus your marketing efforts.

Generally, segmentation is based on factors such as:

Geography

Where do they live?

Where do they work?

Demographics

Gender

Age

Level of education

Occupation

Income

Behavior

What is the primary reason they would use your product or service?

What appeals to them about your brand?

What are their usage rates of your product or service?

Where do they typically source information about your type of product or service?

Lifestyle and values

What is their family situation?

What do they value in their lives?

What are their hobbies and interests?

Do they have children?

Do they have pets?

Your target market should have a need for your product or service and be willing to pay for your offer.

Step 3: Identify your unique selling proposition (USP)

A USP is the unique reason your customers buy from you and not your competitors – it's what makes your business stand out from the crowd. It is important to define what you do differently and be able to convey that to potential customers. Commonly, this reflects your special knowledge or skills.

Your USP may be having a new or unique offering or providing exceptional service. Start developing your USP by answering the following questions:

What do you love most about your products and services?

What special skills or knowledge do you have?

What makes your customers come to you instead of your competitors?

How do your customers benefit by purchasing your products or services?

Which aspects do you generally highlight when you describe your business to strangers?

STEP 4

Develop your business brand!

Every business, regardless of size, is likely to need a brand. A brand is more than a logo, color, or tagline. A well-articulated brand emotionally connects with your target customers and conveys who you are, what you stand for and what you can deliver.

STEP 5

Choose your marketing avenues!

While there are many available, consider your target audience when you are determining which to use.

Options include:

a business website

social media

blogging

brochures and flyers

networking events

print advertising.

word of mouth

cold calling

letter drops.

STEP 6

Set your goals and budget.

Marketing goals will help you to define what you want to achieve through your marketing activities. Your goals should be SMART: specific, measurable, attainable, relevant, and time-based.

You will also need to allocate a budget to your marketing activities. Your marketing budget will need to include elements such as:

- Website development and maintenance.
- Search engine optimization strategy.
- Design of branding
- Printing of promotional material (business cards, brochures, signage, etc.)
- Advertising
- Donations and sponsorships
- Employing staff to undertake marketing activities.

STEP 7

Nurture your loyal customers.

Your customers are the key to your success, so it is important to look after them and encourage loyalty. Providing exceptional customer service can keep people coming back and set you apart from your competitors.

Strategies to build loyalty in customers include:

- Communicating regularly with customers through social media, blogs, or e-news
- Providing after-sale follow up

- Delivering on your promises
- Going the 'extra mile' and providing benefits that exceed initial expectations.
- Using feedback and complaints as an opportunity to improve services.
- listening to customers
- Training staff in customer service and basic sales processes.

STEP 8

Monitor and review.

It is important to regularly monitor and review your marketing activities to determine whether they are achieving the desired outcome, such as increased sales. Initially you should review your marketing plan every three months to ensure your activities are supporting your strategy. Once your business becomes more established review your plan when you introduce a new product or service, if a new competitor enters the market or if an issue arises that affects your industry.

Monitoring activities may include reviewing your sales figures on a regular basis (monthly) or monitoring customer activity during an advertising campaign. You can also access and review free analytic tools to determine the effectiveness of your social media or website campaigns.

All About Loans, Grants, and Contracts

LOANS

Most of the big corporations live off business loans. I suggest that even if you do not need the money, you should still take the loans, if you are approved. The best time to take money is when you do not need it. You can take the loan money and keep it in reserves. This is beneficial for when business is slow. If you have a reserve account, you can still pay bills and employees. This is how many corporations succeed during slow times. Everyone has slow periods in business. So, prepare for it.

Types of loans:

Term loans: Term loans are one of the most common types of small business loans and are a lump sum of cash that you repay over a fixed term. The monthly payments will typically be fixed and include interest on top of the principal balance. You have the flexibility to use a term loan for a variety of needs, such as everyday expenses and equipment.

SBA loans: Small Business Administration (SBA) loans are enticing for business owners who want a low-cost government-backed loan. However, SBA loans are notorious for a long application process that can delay when you will receive the funding. It can take up to three months to get approved and receive the loan. If you don't need money fast and want to benefit from lower interest rates and fees, SBA loans can be a good option.

Business lines of credit: Like a credit card, business lines of credit provide borrowers with a revolving credit limit that you can generally access through a checking account. You can spend up to the maximum credit limit, repay it, then withdraw more money. These options are great if you're not sure of the exact amount of money you'll need since you only incur interest charges on the amount you withdraw. That's compared to a term loan that requires you to pay interest on the entire loan — whether you use part or all of it. Many business lines of credit are unsecured, which means you don't need any collateral.

Equipment loans: If you need to finance large equipment purchases, but don't have the capital, an equipment loan is something to consider. These loans are designed to help you pay for expensive machinery, vehicles or equipment that retains value, such as computers or furniture. In most cases, the equipment you purchase will be used as collateral in case you can't repay the loan.

Invoice factoring and invoice financing: Business owners who struggle to receive on-time payments may want to choose invoice factoring or invoice financing (aka accounts receivable financing). Through invoice factoring, you can sell unpaid invoices to a lender and receive a percentage of the invoice value upfront. With invoice financing, you can use unpaid invoices as collateral to get an advance on the amount you're owed. The main difference between the two is that factoring gives the company buying your invoices control over collecting payments, while financing still requires you to collect payments so you can repay the amount borrowed.

Commercial real estate loans: Commercial real estate loans (aka commercial mortgages) can help you finance new or existing property, like an office, warehouse, or retail space. These loans act like term loans and may allow you to purchase a new commercial property, expand a location or refinance an existing loan.

Microloans: Microloans are small loans that can provide you with $50,000 or less in funding. Since the loan amounts are relatively low, these loans can be a good option for new businesses or those that don't need a lot of cash. Many microloans are offered through nonprofits or the government, like the SBA, though you may need to put up collateral (like business equipment, real estate, or personal assets) to qualify for these loans.

Merchant cash advances: Like traditional cash advances, merchant cash advances come at a high cost. This type of cash advance requires you to borrow against your future sales. In exchange for a lump sum of cash, you'll repay it with either a portion of your daily credit card sales or through weekly transfers from your bank account. While you can often quickly obtain a merchant cash advance, the high interest rates make this type of loan a big risk. Unlike invoice financing/factoring, merchant cash advances use credit card sales as collateral, instead of unpaid invoices.

GRANTS

A business grant is money awarded to businesses in need. Unlike loans, grants don't have to be paid off. The money is not being borrowed. There is no interest attached. Grants are GIVEN to businesses with no expectation of return.

Four types of government grants according to *Amplifund, source reported by: By Rachel Bennett, Head of Marketing October 6, 2020*

1. Competitive Grant – Based on the Merits

Also known as "discretionary" funding, this type of grant is awarded based on a competitive process, which includes proposal selection based on a single reviewer or a team of reviewers. Financing of this type is determined by the merits of the application and is not predetermined.

Examples of competitive grants can include funding for arts and humanities grants, some tuition programs available to students, and scientific research.

Here, it is crucial to understand the grant's criteria to ensure your application is as competitive as possible. In some cases, you may communicate with the organization awarding the funding to have any questions resolved.

2. Formula Grant – Based on Predetermined Award

Unlike a competitive grant, formula grants are awarded to recipients who are predetermined, and the term "formula" refers to the way the grant funding is allocated to recipients. Formula grants, in contrast, are non-competitive.

Legislation and regulations set the formula for this type of funding, so funders must adhere to that formula when awarding grants. Normally, the funds from formula grants are awarded among the States by a specific formula. Next, the choices of which projects to support are made on the local level and funding is recurring. All eligible applicants who meet the minimum requirements stated in the application process are entitled to receive funding.

Examples of formula grants include the Federal governments' contributions to State and local governments for programs such as Medicaid health insurance, education, and transportation infrastructure.

So, what does the formula include?

In short, it is different for every program. This means it's essential that you research the different government agency websites and the authorizing legislation.

3. Continuation – Renewal Grants

Like its name implies, continuation grants offer current award recipients the option of an extension or renewal of existing program funding. This can apply to one or more additional budget period(s) renew grants that would otherwise expire, according to Grants.gov. Depending on the grant program, some can be restricted to existing grantees only, whereas some encourage applications from both new applicants and current grantees.

Because continuing applications often receive priority for continuation funding grants, it's good to keep in mind that if you're a new application, entering a partnership with the currently funded entity could be beneficial.

4. Pass-Through Grants – Issued by a Federal Agency

Under this funding structure, States have the option to distribute these funds as competitive or non-competitive, based on terms and authorizing legislation of the primary award. This gives the State governments both flexibility and autonomy over the use of Federal grant funds.

That said, prospective applicants must keep in mind that they'll need to search and apply through their state's grants office for pass-through grants.

The terms and audit regulations are established by the initial authorizing agency or institution, often referred to as the "prime recipient," whereas the secondary recipients are referred to as "sub-recipients." The prime recipient then issues the sub-awards as either competitive or non-competitive awards dictated by the initial terms and authorizing legislation.

WANT TO GET GOVERNMENT CONTRACTS AND MAKE GUARANTEED MONEY?

Now that your documents for a successful business are set, I suggest you create a sam.gov account. A SAM registration is required for any entity to bid on and get paid for federal contracts or to receive federal funds. These include for-profit businesses, nonprofits, government contractors, government subcontractors, state governments, and local municipalities. In simple terms, this registration is used to get potential contracts with the government. All your business information needs to be correct. As a business you will find that the government has a certain money set aside for small businesses that provide a product or service that they may need. The contracts are endless, and you could even get millions of dollars to do business with the number one customer, the government. You have the option to bid on certain government contracts, some may be 3 -5 years long. This is guaranteed money.

At the time of this book, it is stated that all contractors must be registered in the SAM database. While **you are doing your SAM registration you will be provided with a CAGE CODE and a UEI.** What is a Unique Entity Identifier? The Unique Entity ID is the official identifier for doing business with the U.S. Government as of April 4, 2022. It is a 12-character alphanumeric ID assigned to an entity by SAM.gov. The federal government uses a system called SAM, which stands for System for Award Management.

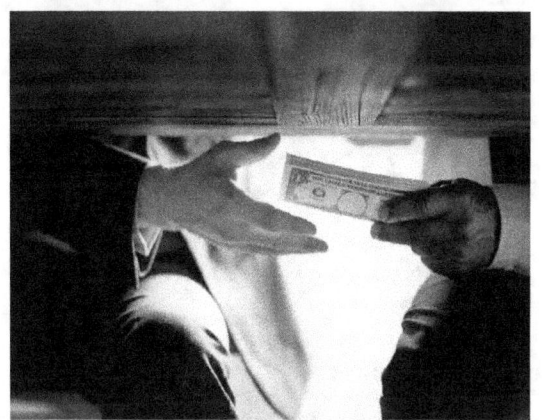

TAXES ARE MADE FOR BUSINESS OWNERS.

Taxes are made for businesses.

In business you can utilize my tax write off to cut paying too much money out. Many business owners use tax deductions to buy land, houses, food, cars, and so many other things. When you are a business, you can get so many tax credits that can help you. As a startup you can also receive up to $5000 in startup cost just for starting a business.

Business requires a stable society to which it should contribute. Business pays taxes on production, people, property, and environmental impact, as well as income. A tax system needs to be crafted to incentivize investment and growth, through dialogue with all stakeholders.

What is a Beneficial Ownership Report? Do I need to file this?

Beneficial ownership information refers to identifying information about the individuals who directly or indirectly own or control a company. This is a new law that has been voted on which will require companies to disclose their beneficial owners to the Financial Crimes Enforcement Network (FinCEN). This Act aims to prevent misuse of corporations and limited liability companies for criminal gain - preventing money laundering, fraud, financing of terrorism, and so on. If you can remember the year 2020 then you may be aware of many people creating fake businesses so they can collect the PPP money which was given out. This left many official businesses struggling to survive during that time. This is most likely why this new law has been put in place.

Who has to file a beneficial ownership? Any company that is created or registered to do business by the filing of a document with a U.S. territory's secretary of state or similar office, and that does not qualify for any exemptions to the reporting requirements, is required to report.

Who is exempt from filing? 23 types of entities are exempt from the beneficial ownership information reporting requirements. These entities include publicly traded companies meeting specified requirements, many nonprofits, and certain large operating companies. I advise you to use your resources to gain more information to determine if you are exempt.

Government Contracting: Unlocking Endless Opportunities for Business Owners

This Photo by Unknown Author is licensed under

Government contracting presents a dynamic and often lucrative avenue for business owners seeking to expand their reach and grow their enterprises. With billions of dollars allocated annually for goods and services across federal, state, and local levels, the government is one of the largest purchasers in the world. This creates a wealth of opportunities for small and large businesses alike to secure steady, long-term contracts.

One of the key advantages of government contracting is stability. Government agencies tend to have consistent purchasing needs, providing reliable revenue streams for businesses that successfully navigate the procurement process. Additionally, many government contracts are multi-year, offering predictable income and a solid foundation for business growth.

On a local level, opportunities abound in sectors such as education, healthcare, construction, and technology. I have personally experienced this first-hand successfully being awarded government contracts with various school districts in my area. Securing these contracts not only provided immediate business opportunities but also enhanced my reputation and opened doors to further local projects.

While the process can seem complex—entailing registration, adhering to regulations, and crafting competitive bids—these hurdles are surmountable with dedication and strategic planning. Building relationships with procurement officials, understanding the bidding process, and demonstrating your capacity to deliver quality work are crucial steps in winning contracts.

For business owners willing to invest in learning the rules and refining their proposals, government contracting offers unmatched opportunities to grow. It can lead to a stable revenue stream, increased credibility, and broad market exposure. With persistence and the right approach, government contracts can become a cornerstone of a thriving, resilient business.

How can you get started in government contracts now!

Government contracting is broken into 3 categories let's look at the breakdown of each:

1. **Local contracts involve: (Easiest Process for beginners)**
    a. Scope: These contracts are specific to a particular city, county, or town. More

for local school districts, community development, etc.
   b. Scale: They are generally smaller in scope and value compared to state or federal contracts.
   c. Focus: They address the needs of the local community, such as local infrastructure projects, city services, or community development.
   d. Registration: Smaller towns may have simpler bidding processes, while larger cities may have their own dedicated procurement systems.
   e. Examples: Local road repairs, park maintenance, waste management services.
2. **State Contracts:**
   a. Scope: These contracts address the needs of a specific state, such as transportation, education, or healthcare within that state.
   b. Scale: They can vary in size but are generally smaller than federal contracts

and more focused on regional development.
c. Focus: They serve the needs of the state's population and infrastructure.
d. Registration: Vendors register through state-specific systems.
e. Examples: State-wide highway construction, university research grants, state-level social services.

3. **Federal Contracts:**
    a. Scope: These contracts involve projects for the entire United States, often with national or international implications.
    b. Scale: They are typically much larger in terms of value and complexity. Example: Providing food, lodging or uniforms to the jails, Military, and government officials.
    c. Focus: They aim to fulfill the needs of the U.S. government.

d. Registration: Vendors must register with SAM.gov (System for Award Management).
e. Examples: Defense contracts, large infrastructure projects, national research initiatives.

Want to get into federal contracting?

- Register your business on the Sam.gov website.
    - You will fill your business information in which will allow them to verify your business. If everything is verified the system will provide you with a **Cage Code.** Once you receive your Cage Code you can begin to source solicitations that interest you. Just search for keywords around your industry or the industry you would like to do business in and submit a proposal.

Want to get started with local contracts or state contracts?

- Register your business on the direct site of the entity you want to do business with.
    - Example: If you are targeting a particular school district you will go to

their site and find the tab on how to become a vendor, or you can look for the procurement tab. Every district has one. Once you find the tab you will put your company information in fillable form and select your desired industry such as construction, youth development, program directions, tax services, school equipment, etc. You can select as many as you want. Once you have selected industries you will get an email letting you know that you are a vendor. You will begin to receive emails for solicitations which you can bid on. **(Read everything correctly and submit your responses before the deadline). Deadlines are strict.**

Keep in mind that you may not win every contract that you submit to, so it's best to submit to many at a time. The government buys everything under the sun. Such as Pens, paper, food, wigs, clothes, tissue, water, different services, Animals, etc.

Terms you should know for government contracting:

RFP (Request for Proposal) A document issued by a government agency inviting vendors to submit detailed proposals to provide goods or services. It outlines the project scope, requirements, and evaluation criteria.

RFQ (Request for Quotation) A document used to solicit price quotes for specific products or services. Typically, simpler than an RFP and used when the scope of work is well-defined.

IBR (Invitation to Bid or ITB) A formal invitation for suppliers to submit a bid to supply goods or services, often used in sealed bidding processes.

Solicitation The overall process of inviting vendors to submit proposals or quotations, usually through RFPs, RFQs, or ITBs.

Bid or Proposal The submission by a vendor outlining how they will meet the government's needs and at what cost.

Contractor The business or individual awarded a contract to provide goods or services to the government.

Solicitation Number A unique identifier assigned to each solicitation or bidding process for tracking purposes.

Pre-Bid Meeting A meeting held before the deadline for bids, where potential bidders can ask questions and clarify requirements.

Award The official selection of a vendor to fulfill the contract after evaluating bids or proposals.

Task Order A specific work order issued under a larger contract, detailing particular services or deliverables.

SBA (Small Business Administration) A U.S. government agency that supports small businesses, often setting goals and set asides for small business contracts.

Set-Aside Contracts reserved exclusively for small businesses, minority-owned companies, or specific categories.

NAICS (North American Industry Classification System) A classification system used to categorize businesses and define federal contracting opportunities.

SAM (System for Award Management) The official U.S. government database where vendors register to be eligible for government contracts.

Subcontractor A smaller business or individual hired by a prime contractor to perform part of the work.

Link to Past Performance Documentation of a contractor's previous work that demonstrates their ability to successfully complete similar projects.

Compliance Adhering to the rules, regulations, and requirements set forth in the solicitation and contract documents.

1099 (Independent Contractor) A tax form used to report payments made to independent contractors who are not employees.

FOIA (Freedom of Information Act) A law that allows the public to request access to government records, often relevant in transparency and procurement.

D-U-N-S Number A unique nine-digit identification number for a business, often required in government contracting registration.

Now that you have all the resources on how to start a legal business, build business credit, and learn about government contracts you are set up for success. Business can be challenging at times but very rewarding. Remember, you are in control of your life, and you are in control of your wealth. Everyone has a gift to share with the world so tap into yours and live a life of abundance.

MY NOTE SECTION:

My Business Name
Is_____
_____
_____

My Business Address
Is_____
_____
_____

My EIN
IS_____
_____
_____

My Business Email
Is_____

_____

_____

My DUNS Number IS

_____

My CAGE CODE IS (Used for government contracting, at SAMS.GOV) _____

My Business Statement
Is_____
_____
_____
_____
_____
_____
_____
_____
_____
_____
_____
_____

_____
_____
_____

Write down any note so you can remember. This could be different business passwords and anything else you may need focused on your business_____
_____
_____
_____
_____
_____
_____
_____
_____
_____
_____
_____
_____
_____
_____
_____

Minding my business written in 2022 by Everett Stephenson

For business consultation email: info@everettstephenson.com

www.ingramcontent.com/pod-product-compliance
Lightning Source LLC
Chambersburg PA
CBHW071213240526
45470CB00018B/1860